AF477418

THE ENDLESS GARMENT

ALSO BY
MARGUERITE PIGEON

Inventory
Open Pit
Some Extremely Boring Drives

MARGUERITE PIGEON

THE ENDLESS GARMENT

A POCKET EPIC IN FIVE COLLECTIONS

A Buckrider Book

Published by Buckrider Books
an imprint of Wolsak and Wynn Publishers
280 James Street North
Hamilton, ON L8R2L3
www.wolsakandwynn.ca

Editor: Paul Vermeersch | Copy editor: Ashley Hisson
Cover and interior design: Kilby Smith-McGregor
Cover image: Freepik
Author photograph: Andrew Querner
Typeset in Calluna and Urbane
Printed by Coach House Printing Company, Toronto, Canada

10 9 8 7 6 5 4 3 2 1

The publisher gratefully acknowledges the support of the Ontario Arts Council, the Canada Council for the Arts and the Government of Canada.

Library and Archives Canada Cataloguing in Publication

Title: The endless garment : a pocket epic in five collections /
     by Marguerite Pigeon.
Names: Pigeon, Marguerite, author.
Description: Poems.
Identifiers: Canadiana 20210253878 | ISBN 9781989496374 (softcover)
Classification: LCC PS8631.I4769 E53 2021 | DDC C811/.6—dc23

FOR NICK KAZAMIA,
ONLY EYES FOR HAIR

CONTENTS

PRE-SEASON

This old thing? I've had it *forever*.
Handmade, yes. 100% natural
yarns: dew retted, decorticated
flax bast; beaten cotton steeped in crocks
of stale urine and indigo; plucked French
angora; hemp bundles; baby Bactrian hair
hand spun on a drop spindle
– it's all organic.

And you wouldn't believe the workmanship.
These artisans who ply weft on a backstrap
loom all day, beat tapa from bark, drape thick
gold velvet brocade into airy shapes like poets
with pins, render culture from memory.

Flowers brought to bloom on the body
by their homey tools: snowflake lace
from Irish spangled bobbins, linens
from vast Egyptian tubs, pompoms
from Mémère's knitting notions.

I like the feel of all that effort. I do.
But it's gotten hoary – démodé.
History's household drudge. Thumbs
working wood or bone, woven clasps
or rope sash, necks struggling through
hemp cloth, hide or silk.

Rigid guild recipes for woad blues
Turkey reds, blends of ochre and soot;
rubrics for who gets what motif,
waking knowing what you'll wear.
Eyes on immediate others, the group nodding –

cloth as conduct   cloth as covenant
cloth as currency   cloth as bastion
cloth as battle cry   cloth as lore
cloth as mirror   cloth as matrimony
cloth as trance   cloth as transmission
cloth as mutation   cloth as name

– the heft of that, of how and who you can be.

To me? Old hat. I want air, to unclasp,
turn out my own looks, eyes everywhere,
free to sample newness, with credit to me,
to whatever's helped can tradition.

Credit circulation, a sitter's collar cut
in medieval miniature poached from afar.

Credit crossover, Renaissance armour
transposed to suiting, butching chests up.

Credit rearticulations by standing loom,
corsetry, touring actors, ambitious cocottes.

Credit the squinting envy of labour: mud
splatter on muscle, harmony in dungaree.

Credit trickle-down style: sobriety in cassock,
allure in criss-cross wraps pegged to Greek statuary.

Credit classes of European wives
whose colonial daydream petered out,
clocks reset by dress orders for boudoir caps,
morning jackets, tea gowns,
layered underskirts, baleen boning
to keep spines erect by evening
in fluted rebuke to any local measure
of the hour.

Credit surplus, winner take all,
raw materials so lush they hallucinated
waste, the tightening mesh of law, of trade.
Missionary, overseer, displacer.
Fordist punch, bent back, cash register.
Portal, cart and checkout,
up to algorithms of preference.

I carry their tribute lightly,
a thought unattended to, gift card
from the unseen whose assigned value
never expires, which I zip into wallet,
toss into tote, forget.

So chuck it all. Join me. Let's shop.

FALL/
WINTER

I'm keen to lose the northern town, its frayed river
and pine-needle streets, the chipped dresser,
red tights dangling out of reach; the church
statue's grey-cast robes; the school's beige brick,
knee skids over gravel stone, every recess
someone teased in flood pants or faded dyes;
hand-me-down hours startled by the bell,
ten after.

Forget how it's mostly February there.
Forget the whispers of snowsuited thighs.
Forget orange Cougar boots marching glum red
tongues single file up crusted snowbanks to fling
insult from sopping home-knit mitts.

I'll keep just this bedialed cathode-ray tube,
rushing home to its brilliant impressions,
jumpsuits unzipped for a Leather Tuscadero effect;
Solid Gold lamé bras; Christmas Snow
hot pants ajiggle with each snort;
waist-tied gingham on shipwrecked Mary Ann;
Starsky leathers and crotch-distressed jeans.

And Main Street, through the drugstore glass:
the magazine rack where my favourites
appeared late every calendar month
(media menses).

Go in. Roam the covers. Choose one mag,
one face, two *smizing* eyes. Watch pixels
and cutlines emanate, dandelion fluff ultralight,
seed pods for instant femininities floating
our way, catching.

That's how I became *Sassy*. A bit *Seventeen*.
Sometimes *Mademoiselle* and *Vogue*.
Inside the gloss, fashion's perfume-sample
essence peeled open and rubbed hard against me:

Her too-small, jewel-embellished bustier,
bared collarbones, Paris bistro, wine
and Gauloises, apt to expose a nipple
in a burst of enthusiasm?
I was that way.

Her thigh-length boot high-kicking romp
through brilliant greenscape, witty top hat
tipped over one eye, pleated skirt lifted,
evoking Scotland, brash fun, pageantry?
These became mine.

Her synched silk trench, vastly oversized shades,
power purse, pencil skirt and blazer,
hailing Manhattan yellow cab, airport-bound?
That was my haste.

Hold those Vaseline worlds,
designers who rectify, photography
safety-pinning feeling, ever-fresh
September issue a ticket out
past the town sign, an odometer's promise,
a transmission tower's enticement away.

Pick up a couple glossies.
I'll order the ride share.

Classic French make. Custom
leather interior. Driver: take my reader
and me anywhere we can shop.

But she doesn't seem to hear, speeds
the wrong way like a woman pursued.
Aren't you someone we know?
Coco. Coco Chanel. And this: Paris.
Are you – we – really here?

> *Style transcends.*
> *I shadow its spectacle,*
> *thread through …*

A pinch of red lips over thin cig,
pending pearls on bouclé knit,
patent-leather toe to gas and a top note of N°5?
It can only be Mme. Chanel. (Achoo!)

Selfie snaps; lapse into her smooth ride.
But, Coco, do you play chauffeur?

> *A stitch of folksiness*
> *is my feu rouge. I halt,*
> *convert what drags*
> *through dirt into clean lines.*

Us folk? Whose drag? (… sniff …)

Deaf again, Coco sets a manic course,
snakes the swollen Seine coughing
exhaust, monologuing about how

she birthed the twentieth century,
she modernized women's dress,
knew how well men's tailoring would suit,
what freedoms thinness would buy.

Lancing heart notes (blink-blink)
as a vaporous reek of memory infuses her breath:
Nazi missions, vicious rants, one bid
to aryanize her prized fragrance.

Coco (cough), I think we're allergic
to your signature formula.

Our driver whips round to glare,
screeches to a stop. Her stick legs poke
from the car door, eau de parfum's
woody base now a throbbing spell

she uses to coax us into a workshop,
where she hangs tailor's scissors from her neck,
unbelts our gear,

sets to work conjuring a dress from air,
stylus fingers edging thighs, armpits,
draping jersey as she mumbles behind
straight pins.

> *We must follow fashion*
> *even when it is ugly.*
> *Erase eras of flounce.*
> *Kill the hocus-pocus of originality.*

Reader, see Coco's vision materialize.
Platonic lines of Beauty, Money and War
hemmed to our very flesh, bullying
what was ours into hers: a uniform of tall,
of lean, pert breasts and pageboys,
urbane stare, desirous mouth.

Coco cracks a grin, satisfied.
But a pinprick to the lip makes her yelp,
rush back to the car in a flap,
hounded by visions

    her cuffed patois inside convent walls
    a provincial stage, men's hot breath out back

from glove compartment she pulls
morphine and syringe, readies and shoots,
jolts the wheel, peels away
faster and faster, fleeing

    nuns
    commies
    competitors
    Jews
    disloyal servants
    birthday candles
    needling names of the dead

On the passenger side, festooned
in Chanel dress, N°5 hooks like a burr.
We try hanky, window crank, bronchodilator
– but this rank odour! Coco, we need to breathe,
have to shop. Please. Give us air.

The designer pushes cigarette
into car lighter, blows opulent smoke,
relaxes.

> *Go? But my modern*
> *is absolutely everywhere.*

Paris melts – gum on pavement
– replaced by this soggy Western strip.
Ping. My app assembles a mood board
from fashion's archive. I've got:

Grace Jones: Whose razor-cut flattop fade. Whose bared teeth.
Whose riot. Whose hula hoop soul.

Rei Kawakubo: Whose lumps. Whose democracy in polyester.
Whose holes for holes' sake. Whose art-world droop.

My aunts Bernice and Shirley: Whose impartial hats.
Whose strategic bangles. Whose NDP. Whose get-up-and-go.

Dolly Parton: Whose dimple. Whose by dint of.
Whose patina. Whose many-coloured throat.

Denise Huxtable: Whose faceted brooch. Whose patchwork pillbox. Whose sly saying-not-saying. Whose echoes.

Patricia Highsmith: Whose instinct. Whose bang. Whose button-down. Whose cigarette. Whose menace.

Prince: Whose high collar, frill, trill, thrill. Whose nude recline. Whose assless squiggle-patterned jumpsuit in sunflower yellow.

Look up. Among low-slung stucco storefronts,
a fabric store stuffed with materials
to bring any look to life. Let's peruse
its bolts – recast cloth as three-dimensional
quasi-bodily realities. How hard can it be?

Just inside, a stray spool of red thread
at my feet. I pick it up, turn it, am instantly
filled with foreboding, its need to unburden
like fresh typewriter ribbon, imperilling
– as if thread could spell out slack secrets,
while, there, along shelves of
Butterick and McCall's, old grudges unfold.

Shed skins of female hands that trailed
tissue maps, indentations from teeth that bit
through tense filament as others snapped out
orders to make more: the needy child,
the luncheon, the engagement party,
the impatient star, the husband, the corpse

all eager to yank away our gift card,
moody icons of the past binding us with thread,
flesh bulging unflatteringly, crossing breasts,
gagging, bloodying corners of the mouth,
thumb and forefinger straining to work free,
to loosen, regain control ...

I put back the spool. We exit the shop.
That whole space a requiem to the darn!
The quilt! The fading idol! The drop-waisted
confirmation dress handmade
in an under-heated vestibule belonging
to that seamstress your mother knew.
Leave it behind. We have places to be.

At the corner, a sandwich-boarded teen,
leaflet in hand, calls to any and all: "McQueen
Ready-to-Wear! McQueen! Mawk-*weeeen*!"

I can't quite believe fashion's games
of time. But who minds? Let's hurry.
The show's about to begin.

Autumn 2009. Backstage, Lee McQueen
composes his haute nightmare: tints
models' brows, presses over lips distorting
red-black plastic ovals; thickens alabaster
face powder, midnight enamel polish;
pins double-tall umbrella hats; saran-wraps
foreheads to a fearsome gloss; draws high
and zips closed hoof-toed feathered boots;
tugs on ruby-studded chain mail balaclavas;
levels stiff, feathered cowls; hangs golden
skeleton keys from ankle straps; fluffs
crimson taffeta skirts whose houndstooth
print dissolves into starlings that swoop
to peck a hem's hidden cursive.

Thinness and tension in elbows, at necks,
kneecaps and ankles; in weaves, darts, seams.
Amidst London damp, Cockney, coke, fame,
fat wallets and falsies, front-row chatter plunged
in a goth swell of drum and bass as, chins up,
the models walk – don't rush

don't think
don't blink too often
don't smile
don't flounce
don't disappear
don't trip
don't waver
don't ask
don't enjoy
don't hate
don't mince
don't mug

don't move so much as reveal passerines
on approach – allow gowns to caw cacophonous
complexities, display extremes of line.

The model, Barthes said, is stemware
empty of all particular taste, an invitation
to the viewer to pour in expression
(wine, poison), signposts to garments,
the model's only duty to

Hold It There.

We are all models, ready to appear
at the tip of this catwalk of feminine being
emptied of all previous words, refracting
designer tales, bodies exalting in present tense,
altered in clothes, ferocity in flesh, coins
minting with each pose, a conspiracy of fabric
and design to make surface of depth:
we belong here.

This runway, locale of ritual and reassignment,
exclusivity and class, binds the clock's hands,
becomes one, as camera clicks parse its dense stretch.

We totter forward, show the season's cuts,
accept the squeeze of a buckled ceinture
or crushed leather ruffle at clavicle, tease
freedom from constraint.

Lee McQueen, eager to sew up time, knows
history disrobes, exposes thin skin to gales
of machismo, grit settling in cracks,
while design, recombinant, bonds flesh
to the present, forms a ready shield.

Let's side with Lee. Desire from the past
only this clever cut, that sleeve, deities
to enhance our visioning exercise,
flourishes for our show, paper doll getups
tabbed over shoulders temporarily.

At the catwalk's edge, saturation
amid show lights, this wish to multiply,
shutter bursts incanting the spell of glamour,
shot by shot. We spin, show backs,
withdraw in a snap of heels (or wheels).

Not so fast.

Between Lee and us models, a woman appears,
tiny, translucent, her face a great,
un-ridged demesne, blood-red fur stole
dripping sarcasm. She blocks our way.

> *If those pants are the party,*
> *those shoes are the hangover.*
> *I've seen shower curtains*
> *with better tailoring than that dress.*

Joan Rivers, back from the dead,
ascending the runway as a red
clapping icon calls for APPLAUSE. APPLAUSE.

> *Are we in a garage?*
> *Because you look like tools.*
> *Can you remove that stiletto?*
> *I need to stab myself in the eye.*
> *Is this the height of fashion?*
> *With Lee McQueen, more like the weight.*

Boos. A crowd that resists arrest
for claims of fashion misdemeanour.
Joan, sensing a bomb, doubles down
on her act, cosmetics mask hardening,
delivery descending to a scratchy husk,
right distal phalange in bright acrylic
pointed hard:

> *You are all ugly.*
> *You are all empty.*
> *You are all naked.*
> *You are all alone.*
> *You are all screens.*
> *You are all silenced.*
> *You will all die.*

Seated mid-crowd, knock-off artists,
sketching madly, titter. A joke is a joke.

Joan, whose life was writing one-liners,
jerks her mouth into a smug slash, slaps
a brittle knee, knowing she's landed. But we,
the models? Inconsolable. Happy until now
in the throes of fashion victimhood, the bid
for amnesia, for endlessly deferred decay,
conjuring with each step along the moment's
thin strip an envious beholding.

We block our ears to a rising thrum
of acclaim (APPLAUSE)
the shifting crowd becoming Joan buffs.

Lee and his inner circle huddle backstage
in the forgiving clutch of a bump (or two).
Girls pull compacts, take screw-faced selfies,
text little nothings; any self-soothing or bid to trick.

Our solace is otherwise: I lift a pair
of Lee's silver-skull studs – one for my pierce,
one for yours; do as you like with its symbolism.

But listen: Lee, pricked
by Joan's barbs, cries out, conveys a hurt
so deep it collapses dead birds, dead girls,
dead muse.

He knows what makes falcons drop from sky,
what pecks at innocence, what shit mars
picture perfection.

His exclamation folds closed comedic distance.
The ghost of Joan is compelled to vamoose.
Security ushers us back onto the street
where, troubled, we wander
a commercial zone.

Fronting Gap, think: People dislike
studied appearances. (We'll borrow our chic.)
Fronting Holt Renfrew, think: de Beauvoir
was right, elegance is women's work that goes
inside and is wasted. (We can still pull it off.)
Fronting H&M, think: we'll buy only good pieces.
(We wear sweatshop tops; feel blood and sweat
mingle down our backs.) Fronting Chapters, think:
fashion and poetry are a lot alike. (Have we
read more about fashion or poetry?) Barthes
said each instance of dress is an utterance.
(We are not ourselves without our clothes.)

Questions like stones weigh shoppers' bags:
who pounds out fashion's stream
of consciousness? Which lowly scribes wag
its tongue? Who toils, stitch by stitch, to frame
garmentry's syntax? Who, as shoulders cramp,
drawstrings tug, wind tighter, skin of the fingers
aching, palmar hinges chaffed? I know;
don't want to know.

RESORT

A man in butter-yellow buttoned gloves
cuts a fine figure in bespoke tailcoat,
high-collared shirt, primrose breeches,
tights and leather-laced boots.

I recognize Le Comte d'Orsay,
who has walked the century, practises yet the art
of the superficial, meticulously attending to gait,
pant crease, cane handle angle, sock tension,
wrist bend, down to neighbourhoods, intersections
where he can deploy, surpass, bond with any city.
The lifted silken knot of his scarf, his balmed lips
close enough to touch. Let's engage him.

Oh, Comte, you, who have modelled
modelling, whose life is an epic of debonairness,
tell us, what is fashion's root?

    How should I know, chérie?
    I am busy standing.
    The light is exquisite.

But please, since we have this moment,
this city's gone Gore-Tex, and the pleasures
of dress rapidly dim. Help us anchor
our wish for flair.

> *Moi? I prefer to be rather than say,*
> *to outfit, be the orange, a treasure of colour*
> *and shape, a surprise burst of taste;*
> *be the rooster, groomed and calling before the rest;*
> *be the fox luxuriating in the coop.*
> *Why fear appetite?*

A question that begs another.
For I've read that dandies like you
used servants to subtract the soupçon
of over-perfection from clothes, pre-wearing
them to a softer ideal, long hours in the skin
of another.

Whose chic, then? That of footmen
sitting on rough wood benches, rare
perfume wafting from your cuffs?
Tailors whose work was so distressed?
Servants achieving a dandy's famed
distinction? Did they resent or pity a boss
who could so worship style?

> *You would have me apologize*
> *for my ton! Ah, non. Touch this velvet*
> *vest, become lost in its pile. See?*
> *What I – and my staff, yes – helped bring:*
> *clothes taking the body's form then surpassing it,*
> *la mode as the cast of a century,*
> *women holding the reigns of representational*
> *dress. Très sexy. You should celebrate me.*
> *Now, please. I must strut.*

Bowing back to our own era,
searching out our *ton*, we too move along
(though I nicked the comte's scarf), front
a department store, a shopper's comfort.

Yet those very foundations resting on soft
rodent fur, beavers in muddy lodges scenting
castor bait, Indigenous-led hunts,
women bonding strategic alliances,
pelts in teeming canoes upriver to ships
stacked twenty feet high, tipping amid swells,
unloaded, marked up, felted to a satiny finish
to slough London's never-ending rain from
the heads of fashionable men, all long dead;

in Cosmetics (1st Flr) if we sniff a free
scent strip, we will whiff again spring torrents
of European capital criss-crossing the land,
fresh-broken ground of dry goods sellers,
blackfly tree stump storefronts sprung
dandelion-thick, followed by sturdy shacks
lining new avenues.

Shadows along the walls of hand
signage, paint drip-drying on plywood;
among the racks, traces of the earliest
fashion plates, capots from Hudson's Bay,
woollens tagged at fixed prices, no more troque;

blow-up banners of supermodels underlaid
with focused faces of people who trapped,
cultivated, hunted, wove, patterned, skinned,
traded and embellished the materials of clothes;

faces at gins, on horseback, in tenements,
on stock exchange floors, at riverside homes
and winter camps of Indigenous and Métis nations;

whispering in the store's synth-pop backdrop,
echoes of settler lore, temperance rhetoric;
every wall supported by innovations in metal works,
glassworks; syndicates, mobs, the seething gaze
of workers hidden under caps, organizing leaflets
bleeding ink, rage; by steam, toil, ledgers, trolleys
and trunks; by incandescent bulbs, pattern sellers,
catalogue copy and flyers.

Behind the scenes, the legacy
of colonial trading companies,
of wheeler-dealer big-picture boss men.
Selfridge saying:

> *Imagination urges on.*
> *It is the yeast of progress.*
> *It pictures the desirable.*

The unloosed fetish for dreams. Pleasure palaces.
R.H. Macy's wooden mechanized staircase churning
(with market, like Ferris wheel, amplifying feeling).
Tea rooms. Orchestras of taste. Curtains, tassels,
silk pillows; the late monochromatic Greenhut's
in Manhattan: green stool seats, green purchase bags,
green typewriter ribbons. Emerald city.

And from every vent, along each aisle,
floor by floor, the close air of women's history
– breath of women buyers, women in sales,
women at the earliest pneumatic money tubes
making change fly, women merchandisers,
models, wait staff, managers – salaried,
travelled, single – alongside oglers, hungry
browsers' cheap gloves on glass cases,
glass windows, glass shelving

eyes trained to see desire boxed and neatly
(nearly) theirs, while just outside, other
women kept out, being the "wrong" kind,
having the "wrong" hands to haul these doors,
even those whose work fashioned the clothes;

their spot at the store's perimeter
inseparable from its floor plan: unauthorized,
unaccompanied (undaunted) persons long refused
the purchase of a clean pair of underwear.

Mannequins recline in the store window's
dazzling champagne picnic scene; crepe rocks,
check cashmere mantles, emerald mulberry
bushes hung with jewelled silkworm cocoons.

Did you know silk moths were domesticated
into flightlessness? The larvae get one orgy
of leaves, one white dream, flight's afterimage
spun out sub-molecularly, bio-desire for takeoff
excreted as filament? All before the sericulturist
boils the larvae alive, each cocoon unspooled,
its thread braided with others for a resilience
the market demands.

Such a covetous scene of increasing heat,
longing for lapsed capacities! Our imaginings
form an impulse knotted to need, a bond
engineered between us and the very start of human dress,
the cosmic scope of design leaving me agog.

But feel how we go too far, become
immersed, are erased – memory first,
then blood, our manner, the way garments
have hung, an undoing we accept, that
scrambles our features, removes fingerprints,
dermis peeled until we too are mannequins,
fibreglass smooth, our dreams entwining
with those of passersby, whose hopes slide
over us like shadows.

In defiance of time, Lee McQueen
and Coco Chanel come stumbling by
(hazy from morphine and blow)
translucent ambition up their sleeves;

at our window, gold chains rattling
from desiccated bone, Coco double takes
before our display:

> *This is la mode.*
> *All I ever wished.*

Lee spits in disgust, lunges
brandishing tailor's scissors to slash
the scene, seeking, as the comte,
a sweeter vein of present tense.

Coco, mad eyes, defends what deadens
behind glass till Lee overcomes her
and she concedes, takes his tape measure
with resentful hand as, together, dead
designers pass through glass, enter our diorama,
set about styling, rearrange legs, the tilt of wrists, of heads,
slip over rigid shoulders the finest gowns.

The first, a hybrid eagle-mermaid look
from Lee's final collection (2010): hand-stitched
in gold metallic feathers, curving tight
at the waist before exploding into
an embroidered white tulle tail.

Another from one of Coco's early, hand-sketched
ad campaigns: carefree flapper slip dress
and low heels, six feet of pearls slung
from the neck in an oceanic U, cloche hat
curving over one blank eye, red lip for élan.

They set us in a darker tableau, perched
couture raptors on the low branches
of a tree bedecked with dollar-bill leaves,
then gather up all that's been shed: our flesh,
our gleam, early sartorial bursts, catalogues
of desire, crystalized memory, then air-kiss us
goodbye, careful not to crack teeth against
our fused lips, after which, eternal midnight,
platinum fingernail moon, solid silver
rat flashing in our talon boots, we forget,
let spotlights bounce halogen off
this empty predation.

SPRING/
SUMMER

Time hung up. A sustained purity of display
until, season over, blasé department-store staff
clear the window, Swiffer our detachment away.
We're stripped, propped on the sidewalk,
torsos and limbs stuck with numbered Post-its
to await reassignment.

Two people stop, assess us, leave and return
with video crew in tow. They walk us through
revolving doors, announce we've been chosen
for makeovers. Extreme editing is in order.

They close us into a room surrounded 360 degrees
by mirrors, a paranoid architecture that compels
us to narrate our lack, our skinlessness, ascertain
the logic of ever owning dreck, revulsion attaching
to personality trait, walk, sentiment, polka-dot
sock and slutty top.

The two people return, bursting into our pen.

> *How do you do it – become living clichés?*
> *Collapse entropy and living?*
> *It's baffling, right, Cliff?*
>
> *Pretty much, Trace.*
> *If they were paying attention,*
> *they'd know their true life*
> *is being, well, snuffed out.*

If what they say is true, how to repair?
How so long muddled? I tear at my carapace
and yours, unscrew mannequin parts, limbs
flung into the bin, stand stripped still further,
no better than air, which brings an enigmatic
smile to the lips of the co-hosts. Trace points
to a bulky dress form draped with flesh:

> *Try this skin on.*

> *I think it will elongate your leg, your hopes.*
> *It might lift your chest, your daring,*
> *your belief in being modern,*
> *not some animal forever migrating*
> *seasonal loops, uncertain, hungry,*
> *unclipped fur, tail, ears and nails,*
> *leaky teats, unruly, un-ruled.*

In this skin? To me? You're a bit 2001:
A Space Odyssey, *can slip time, cucumber cool,*
a Kubrick stewardess in white bubble hat
boiled wool tunic and cat eyes
but not like her because you take
the controls from HAL, see?

Imagine: Lasting!

The seconds caught the way women's
hands once grabbed loom shuttles
and forced them back, tightening time
into a weave of the present.

Funny. In this skin I see you that way,
remade, matched by no one but the self
of your choosing. It's you. Get two.

Trace fits us with the skins, marches us
to makeup chairs where we spin as she
scans our features in the lit mirror,
sponges foundation deep into pores,
reflects:

> *Consider the Zen gardener.*
> *She rejects water, breaks only symbolic*
> *sand swells against stones placed*
> *to move the observer who watches*
> *from a distance that guarantees illusion.*

> *Stones are the basis for aesthetic effect,*
> *the way your mouth, eyes and bridge*
> *of the nose make a face from this backdrop*
> *of skin.*

Picture that gardener up early
before sun owns the whole,
enjoying the imposition of her steps,
gravel stones shushing pathetically
in the teeth of her rake.

Now look at my hand: how I bend
badger-hair bristles to sweep emotion
into the hollows of your cheekbones,
erase vascular notes of feeling,
the flush and strain of blood, of age,
bring about even tone.

That gardener? Who rakes in the serenity
she wants? Plucks leaves and insects
from the coloured sand, her achievement
only suggesting nature and calm
as no actual dead bug or leaf can?
She is me. Could be you.

l try to see my essence in reflection,
to believe that with Trace's assist,
inner truth will spark.

Cliff rolls over a cart slotted with blow-dryer,
curling iron, extensions, lifts a section of hair
between fingers, drops it with a headshake
of dismay.

> *If you take away one lesson from today*
> *it should be that hair is important.*
> *Its growth is yours. Its breaking points are yours.*
> *If I shaved it to shame you, you'd be crushed.*
> *If you unfurled it down a tower for me,*
> *your scalp wouldn't flinch.*
> *If you closed trim in a locket, anyone clutching it*
> *would feel your power.*

Hair is your renewal, your shelter,
your statement, your reveal,
your signature, your capital.

Its colour. Its curl. Its shine.
Its wave. Its thin patch. Its split ends.
Its highlights. Its shaved side.
Its thickening in pregnancy,
loss to healing drugs.
These are all important.

On the orders of our makeover experts
we throw ourselves into the department store
searching out clothes to aid revelation – but which?
This basic black dress? What about jeggings?
A bell-sleeved wrap coat with standing
satin collar? High-waisted palazzos?
Neoprene trench? Shredded colour-block
mohair sweater?

I settle on sensible separates,
age appropriate, go-anywhere hair,
soft lip and mascara, a head-to-toe look
that placates the co-hosts, who hand over
their sponsor's loaded Platinum card.

But oh, do you feel this? Sharp jolts
of electricity as the card touches
my fingertips, visions multiplying
in reverse reflection.

Panopticon

Feel my maternal grandmother
in housedress and orthopedics, home-cut hair
fixed and oiled, bobby pins tucking grey,
astride a kitchen chair, finger-tapping Formica.

    Is that *right? Jeeesus!*

Slapping an arthritic knee, heart
an inner kitchen I enter at will,
food enough that we'll never finish:
speckled trout, Acadian crepes,
boiled ham.

Panopticon

Feel my aunt, 5'10", liquid eyes, full lips,
the long straight hair parted dead centre
that felt so right the year she married
in a maroon suede suit to mid-seventies perfection;
at fifty-some, hurt to have become invisible
to men; ten years on, sunken in hospital gown,
snip of clippers trimming brittle toenails.

Panopticon

Feel my father in burial suit, charcoal grey
and brown over loose shirt collar, jacket sleeves
at rest on the casket's puffed satin, a final,
false impression, a professional's second skin,
a man's life, a message to the cigarette pack,
the faded slippers, the lithium script:
you're all dead, soon buried.

Panopticon

Feel your own icons wildly recreating
within you as Platinum gets so hot it drops,
replaced by hammer in hand, this ache
to smash glass, for the high, resonant tings
of critique, our made-over image settling
in shards as the co-hosts, arms crossed, tip
dolly with foot to haul away their damaged
360 view, us rushing the other way.

Please. Pray with me. Let fashion be
elsewhere and otherwise, the freshest fruit
or most redolent still life, be Harajuku,
sapeur, stuff of punk, flapper, goth, hip hop;
of Delhi, Lagos, Moscow and Montreal;
anywhere they explode codes of dress
into rainbows or tears, hand-tie
jigging lures to make the present bite,
compress heady, plain pleasure
into a confident strut.

March with me straight to the perfume-counter
sales associate who'll arc fragrance across our path,
dreamy clouds of provocation, mists of jasmine,
rosewater, citrus, the smell of money. We're here!
We have to try on as much as possible.

We dive into Cosmetics, pause at stations
lined by sharpened colour sticks: Rich Girl Red,
Zen Rose, Abstract Orange. Each counter ad
a face we'd know anywhere. Halle playing Circe
from on high, short-cropped, staring hard,
prepared to destroy all enemies of beauty.
Opposite, a floor-to-ceiling banner of Charlize
as Diana to this teaming wood of huntable deals,
nodding us to checkout.

We step to the escalator rebranded,
Gucci Guilty, YSL Opium riff at the wrist,
rich Shiseido purple over eyes, preppie
Lauder pink on our cheek, blowouts fresh,
then beeline for Shoes & Bags where we
take our time, stroll alongside displays
of expensive and transformative kicks,
what is lowly underfoot given pride of place.

Try on sandals, our painted toes seen anew:
leads in a love story of never-ending summer,
ten cherries on top; or in thigh-high leathers,
encased so tightly we choke out sacrifice; or
in skin-toned toe shoes, a realist triumph,
our very own *Into the Wild*, the sacred border
between flesh and land lightly tested.

Along the wall, shallow, reflective shelves
lined with bags locked into a chain gang
of indulgence: snake or crocodile, big as tubs,
uterine, with several options to grip, to fill,
gestate, turn keys, compact, Advil, Zoloft,
pepper spray into safety, into style.

We absorb a capsule collection in Smart glasses,
gaze into fashion's future while emailing
our moms, doing some banking.
This wrist cuff to measure our reverie.
Yoga pants loaded with touchable tabs inviting others
to press our anxiety.
A pashmina, also a hard drive for storing thoughts,
featherlight, around the neck. Or these insoles,
which release bursts of positivity.
Shades that block rage.
A tie concealing a small dagger.

I could also use a good bra.
Lingerie is up another flight.

Notice the enveloping light as we rise,
escalator stairs that tint pink. Push through
heavy, scented curtains, massive chandelier
above, rose-coloured ottomans, headless
mannequins fitted with boa-feather wings
in violet and venetian. Above them
a blinking neon sign: SEXY.

My hands brush silken displays:
paper-thin black and purple tiger-print
cheekinis; unlined, gauze multi-way
brassieres; see-through chocolate
and raspberry negligees; garters,
tearaways and spaghetti straps.

All the pieces so tiny – you know your size?
It won't be the custom math of tradition
or rigid specs averaged out in the Depression,
agents of the US Department of Agriculture
on thresholds of borough tenements, banging
farm screens, tape measures in hand. Women
giving over the inches of their waist, hips
and busts for food money.

No, this store seems to use its own system,
counted as Ambien is shaken from the vial,
sizes to cool the chaos of bodies, 00, 000
and the rare 0000000000. What's too big
to shut out left uncategorized.

Here's a cute set – tops and bottoms.
Both mediums. Choose a change room.
Let's split up, try on.

A three-way mirror shows my ass in purple,
shows fallout of culture wars,
the underpinnings of iconicism, improving
geometries. Tits turned half moons to flank
centre gore, triangulating impacts of bottoms,
a wink-wink of secret weapons, a near-Mormon
covenant (my hidden advantage), gym culture,
BDSM, Traci Lords, The Hollywood, the offer,
the money shot – deafening ejaculations
against skin.

SEXY SEXY SEXY, said
that blinking sign.

Rearticulating that early peek
at my mother's nude breast, its raw,
pink expression, certainty that I preferred
to skip all ownership of sexual flesh,
a longing to run, nothing to flop on the chest,
any punch to the gut met with the steely
resistance of heroes: Houdini, Bruce Lee,
my brother.

Rearticulating those wobbly betrayers,
unbaked cream scones gumming up
interactions with torso, gym class;
the word bra a wearable suspicion;
how I made myself clasp behind my back
an inheritance, my very own century
of clergy, op-eds, utopians, health gurus,
women's libbers, dress reformers, anti-fashionists,
sober intimates' saleswomen, brassiere burners,
tech nerds fusing nylon blends, layers
of debate and discomfort exceeding the jugs.

SEXY SEXY SEXY goes
the sign.

Rearticulating my first quasi-feminine
underwear, purchased in my twenties,
height of hair removal interest, expectation
of readiness, grab at liberation, overcoming
a dislike for melons, for the word panties;
could desire, could play vulnerable,
could go hot pink, flick it like it's *dirrty*.

SEXY SEXY SEXY,
the neon insists.

Rearticulating alternatives: nineteenth-century drawers,
loose droop of the era when modesty reigned.
Tug on a calf-length linen shift, squeeze it
at the torso under tight-laced corsetry, add four
starched petticoats, a crisp linen cover, larger
horsehair crinoline, underskirt, fitted under-jacket
and muslin hair cap, all movement accompanied
by the audible sssscchhh, ssssccchhh
of an eternally dusty porcelain damsel.

But in the mirror, someone else's angular face,
tight hair part and suspicious brow.
A woollen soul stretching to share breath.

This one I know from early photographs:
Dr. Mary Edwards Walker, the US Civil War
battlefield surgeon, dress reformer, lecturer
and pariah. I've read about the price she paid
for wearing pants to her 1850s wedding.
Was it worth it, Mary?

> *Turn,* she commands.
> *Let's see the getup.*

Scalpel in her transcendent grip,
Mary scowls, begins to snip stitches.

> *I could never bear excess,*
> *told them time and again,*
> *"I don't wear men's clothes.*
> *I wear my clothes."*

Witness to Mary's frustration, I accept her
precise cuts – but, Doc, I read of the retribution
you faced for stepping so far outside your time,
how you wiped spit from your shoulder
at public talks, took the rough-up, the arrests,
ploughed headlong into poverty, lonely death.

Mary, sweating, snips undergarments
with passion, threatens flesh with
sharp scissor tips.

> *I was always in time,*
> *showed the self my Lord created,*
> *earned my Medal of Honor*
> *in the uniform I adapted*
> *so I could bend, amputate*
> *or sew up those boys' tatters*
> *– to me, the only measure*
> *of what was worth the while.*
> *My prize: a clear articulation*
> *of myself. I keep it polished still.*

Yes. It does blind – or is that a halogen bulb?
Either way, I see your valour, Mary,
have also had enough of doll-making duds,
of those old days when bifurcation on women
was sickness and sin. It's just trying on, Doc.
Just for fun.

The layers Mary's cut flopping off now,
leaving me half exposed, discomfort
as my naked shape peeks out, an encounter
with the unyielding, the fleshy and in-time,
when, rapidly, another ghost edges in
to take Mary's spot.

First a leg, then shoulder, a theatrical
leap into full view – oh, it's Gypsy Rose Lee,
the twentieth-century burlesquer I've watched
in YouTube uploads removing stoles
to rhythmic banter. Gypsy floats alongside,
then – can this be? into me? – because I feel
her assist in removing my frothy understuff,
my mouth puppeted as I singsong:

> *When I take it all off*
> [unstring corset with flourish]
> *every inch laid bare, I am water lapping air*
> [shoulder shimmy]
> *part of you wants to dam me*
> [locate feather fan; make strategic use
> over chest]
> *or fling my gates, drain me away.*
> [cast aside; hip wiggle]
> *Well, forget it!*
> [throw hand in air; shake out hair]
> *Who dares divert an Amazon?*

The next moment: silence.
Gypsy – gone the way of Mary.

I stand alone without clothes, open the door,
toe out toward you, reader, find the pedestal
previously occupied by one of those dummy
angels, step on, strike a pose.

Go on, paint me. I'll hold still.

Difficult nakedness. Your eyes trained
with a portraitist's scrutiny.

Start with protruding tarsals, flesh walked
off in tense constitutionals, the twice
applied birth scar, breasts as cups half full.
One shoulder's socialized immunization scar,
torque in the other, forced forward as shield
for mucus-prone lungs.

Thin skin of a second-born; thick hair
of fish-eating Maritimers; nose imported
long ago from Brittany, peak on an oval
face of just-French aspect; heritage acne rosacea
over cheeks, pink mist on a permanently
windy shore.

One eye lower and mostly blind,
brows overtop: double hyphens for lively
French Canadian names. Face could be serious,
confused or relaxed, hard to say when the gaze
won't hold, keeps going inside to track storms,
begin them, fire starters that die to know, to scorch
white paper in pyrographic zeal.

Please. Sharpen your charcoal tip.
Recast me. Vibe on New Harmony.
Invoke Wreck Beach. Dream Scandinavian.
Celebrate Romanticism or deny it.
Whatever. Just validate representation,
filter at all costs, draw me as that wish.

Then pass me your sketchbook
and I'll draw you, make up a story
of what fashions you.

I crave the plainness of white briefs
like the ones over there, clipped
to hangers, neat in a row, sizes XXS to XXL,
a measure of modesty. We'll get a three-pack
and head downstairs.

I hear there are great deals
in the sub-basement.

DIFFUSION

Going down. Floor to floor.
At the very bottom, blank merchandise guide
staler air flickering lights palms tight on
the escalator's black rail. Muster your courage:
someone hulking ahead.

Excuse me, are you security?
Do you work for the store?

The guard doesn't reply, has a square jaw
cinder-block shoulders, an expression of restriction
I've seen before (in movies? exclusive stores?).
What do they sell in there?

Electric buzz. The door swings wide,
three dozen women pour out, touch fobs
to a device in the guard's hand, escalator up
while the same number descend: mirrored
ribbons of distinct faces. Women tap in, slip through
– all except the last, who slows to grip my arm,
guides us past the threshold into a place
completely new.

Not sales at all, but a vast production floor,
raw fluorescent lighting, sewing machines
in rows. To our right, piles two feet high of pieces
precut of a dress I coveted upstairs, its flaccid
half arms, half backs. Please, I say, turning
to our guide, we only came to shop.

Her gloomy stare, hair in ringlets at the cheek,
a low bun, clothes old-fashioned like those
Dr. Mary Walker cut away from me earlier:
heavily embroidered jacket, satin over petticoats …
A bursting geyser of recognition: you're the poet
Elizabeth Barrett Browning, of the Victorian era.

The more I look the more I can confirm.
Elizabeth's face an exact likeness of a nineteenth-century
daguerreotype I've seen in books: sober, learned,
wary, devout and so long dead.

Now her eyes flash our way and she speaks
in what we assume is the Queen's English:

> *Who do you suppose vouched*
> *for you today? Allowed such porous*
> *exchange with the spirits? Who held*
> *in hand the whole pattern?*

You. You brought ghosts close.
Coco. Joan. Gypsy Lee – all of them.
How? Why?

Questions lost in a horn's blare, the women
tugging blue smocks over clothes, sitting,
bending to work at machines. Elizabeth
points, ordering us to

> *Watch.*

For minutes – hours or days – time fed
to droning sewing needles, slow churn
of ceiling fans caked in fabric dust,
buzz of the door, that guard, at random,
in loom and menace, on patrol, the job
of some workers to sew zippers on children's
shorts, someone else to add instructions:

> Close all fastenings.
> Wash inside out 40°; dry promptly.

Elizabeth, who bids us walk the rows,
along walls lined with boxes stacked ten high,
plastic packing under the fans displacing hot air;
amidst parts piles that taunt the workers,
undiminishable despite the machines grabbing fabric
fast; hearing whirs, clicks, tearings and cuts.
Boredom its own sound.

Elizabeth, this isn't our place. You must see that much.

But the poet has found a box to prop
a leather-bound notebook she leans with,
jotting lines – seeds, maybe, of another
Aurora Leigh, her epic on the "woman question"
of her day: whether the fairer sex could write
as men did, cultivate independent minds
and also love.

Watching her flowing cursive I recall
her character, Marian Erle, a "low-born"
heroine, piecework seamstress whose
needle threaded survival.

Elizabeth, have you brought us here as witnesses?
Is one of these workers a new Marian?

They are not fictions. Not spirits.
Not mine to write. This place is not a reference
to our viewing or an aspect of your quest,
but simply a place of work.

Again Elizabeth turns to her page, her labour,
as do the women; I lightly touch the shoulder of one,
young, busy at her machine, who spins. I search out
the name tag: B— B—; blurt out: Ma'am,
do you need our help? Her eyes go hard,
soften, assess:

I watch over trainees,
know the floor.
How well do you sew?

A question that cuts better than Mary's scalpel,
Coco's cloying scent: I can't affix even a button.

A lack B— B— smiles at.

Girls, much younger, ten and eleven,
occupy a rug to one side, pull apart basting of garments
splashed with random words, dismantle textile
sentences.

Fuck God in the Face.
Mistakes Peaple's Make.
It is only of reative funny.

One child, noticing us agape, smiles,
extends a half de-basted patch of cotton.
The name tag reads E— M—.

You want to try?

I wouldn't but nod my head yes in guilt.
Undead Elizabeth, icy fingers on my elbow,
pulls me up.

Sympathy slows her shift.
Impatience doubles her work.

I am sickened but nearly laughing:
surely this is a waking dream,
that we control this child's time!

And what about Elizabeth? I turn her way
seeking sense, her motives suspect, recall
all the sartorial, moral and bodily binds she sewed
into that epic poem: the psychic seams tested
in the author's own life, the Jamaican slave
ownership that backed her gilded childhood,
how she crumpled in her father's iron grip,
her midlife bid for freedom with her lover,
eloping over the Channel, the activist life
in exile among Italian Republicans,
the mysticism that turned life itself diaphanous.

I scream: If you're so certain of how time works,
then why are you in this place too?

> *It's true I lived in many skins: genius child,*
> *sickly charge, sexual awakener, communer;*
> *always the tight lacing together*
> *of disparate strands.*

> *That is why I am here, learning from*
> *what I see.*

Forever a student of these women
who bind, shift to shift, parts
of their own life stories,
no matter the terrible price.

As Elizabeth again scribbles, the workers
create button-down shirts, jeans, A-line skirts,
embellished shorts, cowl-necked blouses, slacks,
sequined tanks, jersey jumpsuits, hoodies, scoop-necked Ts,
gauzy nightgowns, wool-blend blazers, Lycra
leggings, pink things, children's things, sombre
things, trendy things, pricey things, celebratory
things, sturdy things, flimsy things – a mix we
cried out for as shoppers, dizzying now.

Past a narrow enclosure, women and men work
together in an open yard combing out long strands
of human hair to package for resale.

They sweat before a fire used to seal the ends
before hanging locks to dry while, to another side,
among rows of chemicals in bins, boys of thirteen
stir raw hides, others stretching the leathers
to dry, bare fingers in contact with poison.
I catch more name tags of these young people:
D— R—, Q— T—.

Disregard for conditions and time interspersed
by rides on company minibuses, city sprawl
of San Pedro Sula, Guangzhou, Dhaka,
Kuala Lumpur, urban intensity glimpsed
through Plexiglas, shifts punctuated
by sleep in company dorms; migrants,
locals, pregnant women, married women,
single women, nearsighted women,
devout men and women, girl children,
boy children preparing food, cleaning plates
at a tap, in prayer, texts tapped out
and WhatsApped home, shared stories, poor sleep,
hopeful thoughts, organizing meetings,
demands of better conditions, moments
in solidarity, inside jokes, then back
to escalator up, ribbon down, fob into
the work floor where I stand with Elizabeth,
observing. Only observing.

O place of weak light!
O asses in seats, controlled exits!
O nights and days authorized by whim!
O deft hands!
These hours have no give!
These fingers crack!
These people's poetry is unread!

I run here and there, bang the door. With a buzz,
it opens, but it's Elizabeth's face on the guard's bulky body.
I stumble back, fall, scramble away as Elizabeth yells after me:

> *Patience. You will have everything*
> *you want. A way out is near.*

Out? How soon? These stagnant hours,
pooled, putrid waters fed by sweat,
promise never to end.

Until suddenly: a strange sound.
A snap from above. Everyone unnerved.
B— B— on her feet. She pulls up her mask,
yells at those nearby to

    run.

The hypnotized guard, clinging to duty,
orders B— B—'s head down, hands to task,
while around us, sewing needles, oblivious,
keep a-hum, steel going down-up, down-up,
drones in love with their patterns.

Elizabeth turns my way.

    You will see.

B— B— defies the guard, rises
and pulls others up, screaming, *Get out!*
A series of colossal groans. Sewing pieces
slipping everywhere: collars, side panels,
mesh inserts in pea green, midnight black,
sky blue, scattering on the ground.

Upper floors, held aloft till now by garment orders,
the wallets of shoppers, praise of novelty,
the need for jobs, suddenly find the gravity
of a bench judge whose mallet always falls
with purpose, smash verdict on everything below.

Not enough doors. On the windows, heavy bars.
Workers yanking anyway, wild gestures,
silent film actors awaiting the yield of props
the director to yell CUT.

The department store crashes down
onto the factory floor, women, children, men
now ingredients forcibly swirled into
rising beige debris.

Down come fur coats
Down come cash drawers
Down come blasting hand dryers
Down comes a rain of perfume bottles
Down come tube socks, stretched or rolled into cotton question
        marks
Down come the people: clerks, sales managers
        retirees still clutching teacups from the store café
Come booties, come men's shirts
Come gloves like waving hands
Come mannequin arms and legs.

Workers, including B— B—, alive
in pockets of dwindling air, dial cellphones
out, reach loved ones in sane places:
restaurants, markets. Factory voices
choke out

> *save*
> *help*
> *love*

Great stacks of garment parts howl
through forked tongues of uncut zippers.
Sewing machine needles leap like hornets
to stab, sew to walls, embroider with doom
attempts at escape – every single one.

Except ours.

Elizabeth walks calmly to a crack in the floor,
without hesitation steps in, tips down, back shoe
the last we see of her before I overcome paralysis
to rush over and leap with her – you can jump too,
fall with us as feathers from a bird, silently and long

soft landing on what feels like rubber
but putting down hands to stand,
the surface sticky, wobbly, deep red, a-throb,
stretching north, south, east and west
while above, the crack closes without
letting out another soul, the entire scene
sealed into a dim ochre sky.

Is this hell? I ask. Punishment for the weight
of fashion? The tangle threading garments,
their making, my ego and my wearing?
Between us and our dreamed selves? Between
words and experience? Please, Elizabeth!
Hold me up or I'll sink into this red muck,
into despair!

Elizabeth, anger conveyed in her
rigid grip, sets me standing.

> *No need for dramatic turns.*
> *No more words.*
> *Here she comes.*

Look – to our left. Listen as the goo puckers.
Something is rising there. A small column
that differentiates itself into girlish shape,
hair of blood, blood for a face, blood from fingertips,
a creation entirely of blood, but organ-like,
alive with heart, half my height, one raised
protrusion pointing.

I recognize right away E— M—,
the girl from the seam floor. She is sombre,
points to a path where headstones have formed
from the red, the nearest with names she speaks aloud:

S— ... L— J— ... V— ...
E— M—. That one's mine.

Farther on, much older graves, each
carefully inscribed. The girl points
again and again, speaks each name
in a garbled tone:

M— L— ... F— V— ...
R— C— ... Y— B—

I turn away, would lean against Elizabeth's
black dress except she forcefully pushes me back.
I try to make out E— M—'s girlish features
but they've blurred. Why were you working?
You're only a kid.

*Forget all that. I can tell you
that I always loved hair.
I bought very pretty barrettes
with my pay.*

*If you had known me, before,
I might have given you one.
I liked to do braids. My hair still grows,
but it's kind of gross. Can you help?*

Help? But we are guilty. We slowed your work
with our hurry, bought the clothes that ...
Besides, we're stuck here, like you.
Can't you see this is hell?

E— M— tilts her head, consternated.

*I don't like you to use
that word.
Just untangle it, will you?
It gets all knotted.*

I recall our time upstairs, Cliff's rant:
"... Hair is important." From E— M—'s extended arm
comes a wide-headed brush, which I take
and apply, run through with difficulty,
blood leaking to the ground.

> *Ah. Nice.*
> *No one has done that since ...*

I press the brush, really get into it,
use my hair elastic to secure a ponytail.

> *Better. This gives me a new feeling.*
> *Or an old one.*
> *Does it give you something new?*

Her form collapses into the landscape of ooze.

Please! Come back.

But Elizabeth, hand to my shoulder,
guides us farther across the plain.

A wide cliff overlooks a sloshing red sea.
A funeral is underway, goopy bent figures
standing over an open grave.

They wear clothes of different times,
of Elizabeth's, of mine, of many lands
and peoples; black suits, white shawls,
red blankets, pleats, stones and togas.

The one officiating speaks.

We called our beloved: maker,
weaver, knitter, embroiderer.
You called her, him or they: mother,
daughter, brother, father,
cousin, tailor, guide.

Celebrate these designations,
every seam sewn, button secured,
prom dress frilled, volleyball shorts hemmed,
baby sock knit. Each heirloom kimono,
each couture gown, each cheap shirt,
all the schemata – things made.

So many fresh graves. So many lying
forever here in the name of fashion
who also had style, who also doubted,
who also journeyed, wasted now
in the name of change,
of what is modern and new.

The funeral erodes. A host of stones appears
where the mourners have just stood.

Here lie courtiers whose lead face paint
took their brows, hair,
then minds

here lie wigs so tall
a child holding a support had to follow
the duchesse through the party

here lie mad hatters,
whose mercury-poisoned hands
felted unfathomable chapeaux

here lie shirtwaists before the inferno,
clogging discount tables
at New York department stores

here lie bolts of fake suede
never to become hippie hot pants
because one season late

here lie plaid, bell-bottom polyester
slacks whose material
has not decomposed one bit

her lie plastic pieces
of bygone sneakers from
a thousand Jane Fonda workouts

here lie T-shirts grown men and women
threw out without wearing once,
tags still on

here lie truckloads
of fast fashion the store
slashed and chucked, New York, 2013

here lies H&M overstock
incinerated into ash, USA, 2018

here lie runway couture pieces
airtight in plastic, withheld from sale
to prop the brand

here lie stacks of Vogue captions
on last spring's must-haves
in a mass grave of text

here lie digital files of selfies
from Kardashian-style Insta posts
from last month but long dead

here lie participation Ts for fun runs,
bank promos, charity cleanups
and viral sensations

here lie swag bags
for reality TV shows no one
bothered to watch.

Used clothes form the rising terrain upon which,
for days or years, we clamber and trip, up a mountain
of gunky sweaters, until we come to a ladder.

> *Have you seen? asks Elizabeth.*
> *This territory of materials and trends,*
> *bodies and independent minds,*
> *exploitation and adaptation,*
> *can be mirrored in conscience – theirs,*
> *God's, yours, mine – or go untraced.*

> *I impressed feelings and thoughts*
> *into the mouths of poems, landed in a place*
> *not of sinners or mystics, but of grief,*
> *of blood that flows in every vein,*
> *every verse.*

> *So have you seen?*

I think so, I say, my foot on the first rung.
I turn to ask you the same, though
I await no answer as joy lifts my aching legs up.
Just follow. We leave – now!

Elizabeth's long skirt a shrinking black sphere
beneath us; above, a hinged trap door,
which we push back, emerging into a space
so glaring my eyes burn.

A change room without a door.

In the mirror, my Chanel couture,
the comte's scarf, Lee's skull earring,
my Smart glasses and blown-out hair.
The web we've passed through,
been caught in.

A scene takes shape in the glass:
a schoolroom full of young children.
Lean forward with me, look through the windows,
watch as kids start their string game, fingers
through long loops with knotted ends that E— M—
might have liked: pinch out, pull through,
tuck and tug; make Butterfly, Witch's Broom,
Eiffel Tower, Star, Saucer, Cup.

The picture fades as another sharpens:
a busy street – any city, anywhere –
a garment's train dragging down the sidewalk,
its ripples a dissonant refrain stretching
to overtake square footage, avenues,
acreage, neighbourhoods, countries, bodies.

I'd like to stop, I say aloud, though no one
can hear but you. No one halts the garment
– until, suddenly, everything is gone
but the view we have of ourselves
and I do know something new:

we will stay in this spot, dressed for life
in reflections of what we try on, add to,
tear, mend, wear in myriads of ways, stitch
grafted to skin, preference patching
battered weave until what looks back
has been taken in, hemmed to convey
less and less, words like popped buttons,
undone to our least modern avowal.

NOTES AND ACKNOWLEDGEMENTS

This book's title derives from chapter 4 in *The Fashion System*, by Roland Barthes, translated by Matthew Ward and Richard Howard (New York: Hill and Wang, 1984), 42–55.

Two research titles were touchstones: *Women's Work: The First 20,000 years*, by Elizabeth Wayland Barber (New York: W. W. Norton, 1994), and Anne Hollander's *Sex and Suits: The Evolution of Modern Dress* (New York: Alfred A. Knopf, 1994). Epics that I returned to for help were Elizabeth Barrett Browning's *Aurora Leigh* and Gwendolyn Brooks' *In The Mecca* (New York: Harper and Row, 1968).

Thank you to Paul Vermeersch and Noelle Allen, without whom this book simply would not be. The poets Rahat Kurd and Chris Hutchinson, as well as my brother, Jean-Claude Pigeon, read the poem with care. I thank them for their time, notes and insights.

Sections of the book were published in earlier forms as *What I'm Wearing Now* (North Vancouver: Alfred Gustav Press, 2017); *My Model Poem* (Vancouver: Nomados, 2017); *Cuttings*, with artist Birthe Piontek, accompanying publication to her solo exhibition, *Miss Solitude* (Kimberly Phillips, Curator, Access Gallery, 2017); and *From the Endless Garment*, in collaboration with artist Fabiola Carranza (*ti-TCR: a web folio* 14, 2016). I thank the editors (David Zieroth, Meredith and Peter Quartermain, and Matea Kulić), artists and curator for encouraging my writing.

The Canada Council for the Arts provided funding assistance, for which I am grateful.

The idea for this project came up during an enlivening conversation with Adam Frank in Montreal in 2012. So much enlivenment has followed. I thank him and my kids, Merle and Lewis, for it all.

MARGUERITE PIGEON writes poetry and fiction. Her previous books are *Inventory* (Anvil Press), *Some Extremely Boring Drives* (NeWest) and *Open Pit* (NeWest). Untangling her arm's-length preoccupation with clothes has been an odyssey. Spiritually northern Ontarian, she lives on unceded lands of the Musqueam, Squamish and Tsleil-Waututh nations (Vancouver), where she works as a freelance editor and writer through her business, Carrier Communications.